My Five Super Senses
I TASTE IT!

Theresa Emminizer

PowerKiDS press

I taste my breakfast.
I like it!

I use my mouth to taste things.

I taste the ice cream.
It tastes sweet!

I taste the lemon.
It is sour!

I taste the tea. It's hot!

I taste the water.
It's cold!

I taste the watermelon.
It's juicy!

I like the taste
of apples.

There are some tastes I don't like at all.

The food I make myself tastes the very best!

There are so many things to taste!

Published in 2024 by The Rosen Publishing Group, Inc.
2544 Clinton Street, Buffalo, NY 14224

First Edition

Editor: Theresa Emminizer
Book Design: Rachel Rising

Photo Credits: Cover, p. 1 Eduard Stelmakh/Shutterstock.com; p. 3 wavebreakmedia/Shutterstock.com; p. 5 Skydive Erick/Shutterstock.com; p. 7 Jacob Lund/Shutterstock.com; p. 9 bluebeyphoto/Shutterstock.com; p. 11 Pixel-Shot/Shutterstock.com; p. 13 fizkes/Shutterstock.com; p. 15 Fernanda Flugel/Shutterstock.com; p. 17 Markus Mainka/Shutterstock.com; p. 19 TheVisualsYouNeed/Shutterstock.com; p. 21 Lordn/Shutterstock.com; p. 23 New Africa/Shutterstock.com.

Library of Congress Cataloging-in-Publication Data

Names: Emminizer, Theresa, author.
Title: I taste it! / Theresa Emminizer.
Description: Buffalo : PowerKids Press, 2023. | Series: My five super senses | Audience: Grades K-1
Identifiers: LCCN 2023028406 (print) | LCCN 2023028407 (ebook) | ISBN 9781499443417 (library binding) | ISBN 9781499443400 (paperback) | ISBN 9781499443424 (ebook)
Subjects: LCSH: Taste—Juvenile literature.
Classification: LCC QP456 .E46 2023 (print) | LCC QP456 (ebook) | DDC 612.8/7–dc23/eng/20230712
LC record available at https://lccn.loc.gov/2023028406
LC ebook record available at https://lccn.loc.gov/2023028407

Manufactured in the United States of America

CPSIA Compliance Information: Batch #CWPK24. For further information contact Rosen Publishing at 1-800-237-9932.

Find us on

PK Beginners

Titles in This Series

I FEEL IT!

I HEAR IT!

I SEE IT!

I SMELL IT!

I TASTE IT!

ISBN: 9781499443400

9 781499 443400

PowerKiDS
press

YOUR LUNGS

George Fittleworth